Contents

Published and printed in the United States   ıy
Kalamazoo, Michigan 49001 (

Publisher's representative for distribution in Canada. Horta Craft Ltd., London, Ontario.

ISBN 0-89484-001-0

Introduction

Hanging plants add new dimensions to the indoor and outdoor scene. A great variety of plants make ideal hanging subjects: attractive displays use not only the natural trailers like English Ivy and Wax Plant, but also plants with spreading habit such as the Prayer Plant; cascading, drooping types like ferns and Spider Plant; and rosette plants like the African Violet as well as the more erect forms of Japanese Aralia and flowering Azalea.

Suspend your living accessories at any level to suit your tastes as well as the plant's needs. With hanging plants, tables and countertops remain uncluttered—and your favorite plants can be safely out of the reach of children and pets. And where space is limited, hanging gardens may be the *only* way to use plants.

The shade loving ivies, Waffle Plant, and Philodendron brighten dull corners and hallways; an herb garden suspended in the kitchen adds flavor while leaving all your work surfaces clear; brightly lit spots are great for the Strawberry Begonia, English Ivy, and Purple Passion Vine; and flowering plants like Browallia and Petunia enjoy full sunshine, indoors and out.

Care instructions accompany the illustrations throughout this book, and the next few pages contain some additional details to help you enjoy long-lived hanging plants.

Acknowledgements

Hanging Plants for Modern Living contains a broad selection of all types of plants for use in hanging containers. There are more than 110 full color illustrations of many different foliage plants, of ferns with their naturally cascading fronds, of vines and ivies, plus several flowering varieties, all in use as hanging plants. Indexes of common and botanical names are included in addition to the section on general care of the plants: this covers light and temperature needs, watering, fertilization, and a diagnostic chart for many disorders of indoor plants.

Photographs are from Merchants comprehensive library of horticultural subjects; this collection of over 10,000 pictures has been compiled by horticultural photographers John Pike and the late Willard Kalina.

We thank the following companies for their kind assistance in providing material and some additional photographs for this book:

Arvida Nurseries, Miami, Florida; Geo. Ball Co., Chicago, Illinois; Bamboo Nurseries, Inc., Apopka, Florida; B. L. Cobia, Inc., Winter Garden, Florida; Daisy Farm, Miami, Florida; Dickerson Greenhouse, Bloomingdale, Michigan; Fantastic Gardens, Miami, Florida; Hattaways, Inc., Altamonte Springs, Florida; Riverside Greenhouses, Kalamazoo, Michigan; Specialty Crafts Co., Houston, Texas; Tri-Tiki Nursery, Winter Garden, Florida; Van Bochove Flowerland, Kalamazoo, Michigan; Walters Gardens, Zeeland, Michigan; Weber Bros. Greenhouse, Inc., Oak Park, Michigan.

Copy for the book was prepared by M. Jane Coleman, PhD, technical writer for Merchants Publishing Company. Guidance and assistance is acknowledged with thanks to Charles A. Conover, PhD, Director of the Agricultural Research Center in Apopka, Florida.

Time to Adjust

Any living thing that is transferred to a new environment undergoes a period of adjustment. For the plant this usually means becoming accustomed to the drier atmosphere, warmer climate, and reduced light levels in your home. The range of plants available for home use includes many that are well able to thrive in these conditions, though they are often produced in quite different environments.

Initially, the plant's leaves lose water more rapidly than they did when it was growing in the greenhouse, and its roots may not be able to supply replacement water as quickly. This is one reason that the new plant sometimes loses a few flowers or mature leaves in the first week or two. Another cause may be that there is not enough light to sustain all the leaves your plant grew in its previous location, even though subsequently the plant will live and grow well in this new position. If losses continue for several weeks, some other factor should be suspected—see page 77 for more details of plant troubles.

For the first week or two your new plant probably requires frequent watering; spray the foliage every day if possible. It is best out of direct sun, even if it is a sun-lover; and a cooler position (55-60°F) also reduces water loss and thus will help the plant adjust to your environment.

Light and Temperature

There are plants for shady and light places, plants for warm and cool places —as indicated in the care instructions on pages 9 through 76.

The different rooms in your home offer a variety of climates, some with lots of sun and extra warmth, some which are always shaded and cooler, and others where nights are usually well below day temperatures. Make use of these differences in plant selection for each location, and enjoy the natural grace of many different flowering and foliage plants.

Light requirements for plants indoors

1. *Full sun* loving plants are good in or near sunlit windows, or in places where there is strong reflected light. These plants frequently like fresh air, though not hot or cold drafts. There are also several plants which enjoy full sun in winter, though the full noon-day sun in summer is too strong. These plants need partial shade during the summer months.

2. *Diffused light* prevails in an average to well-lit position out of direct sunshine, or with a sheer curtain between the plant and sunlight. Such plants are best placed inside the room 4 to 8 feet from the window, or in a north facing window.

3. *Shade* loving plants grow best with indirect light, in dull corners, or more than 8 feet from the window.

Temperature requirements for plants indoors

The temperature ranges given here are those within which plants will thrive and grow: yet plants are adaptable, and even though many do not actually grow when the temperature remains below 65°, they will survive for a long time in cooler climates.

1. *Cool* loving plants grow best with day temperatures of 60 to 70°F, while nights may be as low as 45°. Some of these plants are frequently grown out of doors.

2. *Average* temperature plants need days of 65 to 70°F, and up to 75° in the sun; their preferred night minimum range is 50-55°.

3. *Average to warm* temperature plants really need days of 70 to 75°F for growth, and they will not be harmed by 85° in the sun; nights can fall to 60 or 65°, even as low as 55° for some varieties.

The Hanging Environment

1. It's warmer up there—

The care of hanging plants is little different from that of plants growing in any other type of container. However, hanging plants often use and lose water more rapidly than their surface-bound counterparts. Indoors the air is warmer closer to the ceiling. Air movement all round the plant and its container, both indoors and out, also leads to greater water loss. It's not surprising to find a hanging fern, for example, with dry soil, while a similar plant on a table in the same room is still moist.

2. Trim exuberant growth—

Trailing plants like Wandering Jew, and spreading bushy ones like the Prayer Plant, need regular trimming to encourage branching and vigorous new growth, and to thin overlapping foliage which crowds out other parts of the plant. When your hanging plant is growing vigorously, pruning or trimming will keep it looking the way you want.

3. Hanging plants outdoors—

The majority of plants shown in this book are normally used for indoor decoration, and the full sun recommendation is based on the fact that the sun shines into a room for just part of the day. Outdoors, where the sun may strike the plant for most or all of the day, and where there is much more air movement to dry the plant, shade is usually needed to prevent burning through rapid water losses from delicate plant tissues.

Absolute sun lovers like petunias and geraniums will of course thrive in full sun outdoors as well as inside. In fact, any garden plant you wish can be grown in a hanging container out of doors; but as in any container, root space is limited, and drying out can be very rapid—so be prepared to supply enough water for your plant's needs.

Watering

How often do they need water?

You can tell when the plant needs water by the feel or look of its soil; the weight of the pot is another indicator. The rate at which the plant uses and loses water depends on variety, growth rate, temperature, light and relative humidity. Let the plant itself be your guide to watering at all times of the year; hanging plants tend to need more frequent watering than others, even in the same room.

When the soil surface is dark and damp to the touch, the whole root ball is probably moist — as it should be if you've just watered it (see below). While it dries out, the soil color gets lighter though it will continue to feel moist for some time. The surface generally dries before soil further down in the container, so let the top 'feel' of the soil be your indicator and the entire root ball will rarely dry out.

In care instructions for plants, three different watering requirements are noted.

1. There are some plants that should not be allowed to dry, ever. They can be watered again when the soil surface starts drying, before it gets powder-dry.

2. Most plants for indoor use need to be kept uniformly moist but not wet. The soil surface can be allowed to dry more than those in the first group, and you won't do any harm if the plants sometimes dry out entirely for brief periods. But frequent drying out will cause damage, resulting in leaf losses.

3. Plants such as cacti and succulents thrive when their soil is allowed to dry out between waterings.

How much water should be given?

No matter how often or rarely you water the plant, be sure each time that the whole root ball (all the soil) is thoroughly moistened; and that the excess water can drain out of the container if possible.

A thorough watering followed by a period of time to allow the soil at least to start drying, permits air to be drawn into the root ball. Plant roots need oxygen for life and growth, and if they are constantly saturated by water 'little and often' they will soon die.

Hanging plants can pose a singular problem when it comes to drainage: plan for an overflow from your hanging container, either by the use of a built-in saucer, or by taking the whole plant to the sink or bathtub whenever you water thoroughly, then leaving it to drain well before rehanging it.

The solid plastic hanging baskets usually have a snap-on saucer to catch the drips, so they can be watered in place most of the time. Glazed pottery, metal, and glass containers without drainage holes can also be watered *in situ*, though the correct amount must be added to avoid over- or under-watering the plant. Mesh baskets, those made from wood, bark, and unglazed pottery, as well as flower pots with drainage holes — all drip after correct watering. If the overflow liquid will cause damage, place the plant in a bowl or sink until it has drained completely.

Is tap water OK?

Generally yes, though water from the cold tap may be too cold for the plants. It is best to use water at room temperature; that is, above 60°F, for indoor plants. Either add a little warm water (don't cook the plants!) or leave it to stand overnight so the water warms to room temperature.

Fluorides can be harmful to some plants, specifically *Dracaena, Cordyline* and *Chlorophytum,* in the range of foliage house plants; and similar damage has been noted on *Maranta* (Prayer Plant) and *Agave.* Over a period of time, added fluorides cause brown spots and/or leaf tip burn on the sensitive plants (see page 77 for other causes of similar symptoms).

The quantity of fluoride normally added to municipal water supplies is sufficient to harm these plants. Perlite, a soil additive often used to help soil aeration, also contains potentially harmful amounts of fluoride.

To overcome or avoid fluoride damage:

1. Avoid the use of fluorinated water. Other sources are snow, rain, well- or spring-water (this can be checked by your local or state testing center for mineral content), and dehumidifier-water.

2. Raise the pH (acidity) of your potting soil to 6.0-6.5; in this range the fluorides are relatively unavailable to plants. Repot in soil containing dolomitic limestone, replacing as much soil as possible in the plant's root ball.

3. Avoid the use of superphosphate in your potting mix; superphosphate contains a high level of fluoride.

Chlorine in tap water does not usually harm plants, and if you allow the water to stand in an open container for 12 to 24 hours, most of the chlorine will escape. However, the one exception to the relative harmlessness of chlorine is in misting or spraying fern fronds; as this water evaporates, any chlorine in it will cause browning of the delicate fronds.

Water-softener water will not harm your plants, provided the softening equipment is functioning correctly. This water still contains chemicals, though the lime has been replaced with more soluble compounds.

Soluble Salts—Leaching Hanging Plants

When you fertilize your plants, you add chemicals to the soil; water contains chemicals too, so even when you water them, you are adding to the soluble salt content of the soil. The growing plant does not, nor does it need to, absorb all of these soluble chemicals. They accumulate in the soil. High concentrations will damage the plant, causing loss of roots and subsequent foliage loss, reduced size of new growth, wilting even while the soil is moist, and collapse of the whole plant.

Good watering practices help to keep the soluble salt build-up to a minimum, if the excess water (really a solution) is discarded every time you water. But with regular fertilization and watering, the accumulated soluble salts should be washed out of the soil by leaching at intervals of 2-3 months.

TO LEACH: immerse the container in a bowl of water to saturate the root ball and all the soil; after about 30 minutes, or when bubbles stop rising, remove and allow it to drain. Containers with no drainage holes should be tilted to permit the drainage solution to run out over the edge. Repeat this procedure one or more times with clean water.

Fertilization

Match plant growth

Plants brought into your home from the greenhouse are moving to an environment where light is less intense and hence where growth will be slower. Most plants already have sufficient fertilizer in their soil to sustain growth for up to three months in home conditions. This is particularly so during fall and winter.

Even if your new plant continues to grow vigorously, it is wise to wait a month while it adjusts to its new environment, before adding fertilizer. Likewise, a newly potted plant needs time in which to grow new roots to absorb the fertilizer you'll be applying.

Guidelines for fertilizing each plant are given with the care information on pages 9 thru 76. It is often easier to feed a number of plants at the same time, and the schedules can be combined in this way: for a general practice, apply fertilizer to most indoor plants every 1-2 months while growth is rapid, and once or twice only during the winter months. Alternatively, apply the plant food more frequently in a dilute form; this accommodates plants which would be injured by full strength fertilizer. 'Half the recommended strength' means using only half as much fertilizer per plant or in solution.

Annual plants grow very quickly and need fertilizing every two or three weeks during their short season. Some flowering plants, like Azalea, should not be fed at all while they are in flower.

Fertilizer type

Any prepared mixture for the type of plants you have is fine: for most house plants, an N-P-K analysis ratio that is close to 1-2-1 will give balanced growth. African Violets are best with a mix containing more nitrogen (N); and there are other formulations available for the acid-loving plants like Azalea and Gardenia. For annuals and other garden plants growing in hanging containers, an outdoor fertilizer is fine.

Soluble compounds are easy to apply and show quicker results than solids or slow release pellets. Simply apply the fertilizer solution in place of water when you would normally be watering the plants. However, be sure the soil is slightly damp when you fertilize; never feed plants with dry soil, because roots will be damaged by the chemicals you add unless they are diluted further by soil moisture.

Use all fertilizers at or weaker than the recommended strength of dilution, never stronger. Newly rooted cuttings, seedlings, and young plants will benefit from weaker solutions to avoid damage to the soft young roots.

Planting

The container

The illustrations in this book show a wide variety of different hanging containers, ranging from wire and plastic mesh baskets and suspended flower pots, to choice pottery items with macrame hangers.

A fast growing plant, like German Ivy, or one with naturally cascading foliage like the Boston Fern, needs no elaborate container for it will soon be all but obliterated by the plant. On the other hand, small and dainty plants such as the African Violet or Peperomia, which are often hung below eye level, can be shown off to advantage in a decorator pot which enhances your decor.

Ideas for hanging containers are as limitless as the imagination: macrame supporting a globular terrarium, a birdcage to contain a variety of ferns, a wide-necked jar for plants growing in water, and many more.

Planting

Clay, plastic, wood, metal, and pottery containers can be planted just like any flower pot, with a layer of broken pot or pebbles at the bottom so the drainage holes don't become clogged with soil. For containers without drainage holes, a layer of coarse material under the soil acts as a buffer against overwatering, so roots are not continually in the accumulated water.

Mesh containers should be lined with plastic, or with sheet or sphagnum moss. The plastic will prevent dripping, though you should punch a few holes at the bottom for drainage.

The soil

Information that accompanies the plant illustrations in this book includes a note about the type of soil preferred by each group of plants. It is important for hanging plants that the soil retain sufficient moisture, so you don't have to water them constantly; also that it isn't too heavy.

Generally, the same basic mix can be used for all house plants: this consists of equal parts sterilized soil, peatmoss, and sharp sand. The sand can be replaced with Perlite for reasons of weight, if necessary. The basic mix is then varied to come closer to the content and texture of the soil in which your plant is already growing.

To sterilize your own soil, first moisten it, and then heat it in a covered (not sealed) fireproof dish in the oven. Its temperature should reach 160-180°F (use a meat thermometer if you have one), and remain there for about 25 minutes. After cooling, add the peatmoss, sand, and any other additions you require.

Another good basic mix for house plants is one consisting of (by volume) two parts peatmoss and one part sharp sand. This saves soil sterilization since both peatmoss and sand are already virtually free of weed seeds and harmful organisms.

Mixed Plantings in Hanging Containers

Most of the illustrations in this book show single plants used as hanging items. However, many fascinating and unusual variations can be created by mixing plants in your hanging gardens. A single container may be planted with a mixture of foliage and flowering plants; or with a variety of compatible foliage plants (similar watering, light and temperature needs) for permanent decoration. Seasonal or special attention plants can be added in individual pots, for easy removal. Individual plants may also be grouped on separate hangers at different levels for an exciting garden effect.

Rosary Vine *Ceropegia woodii*

Slender trails of marbled heart-shaped leaves cascade to 3 feet or more. Small tubers on the stem will grow to new plants when planted.

Caring For Your Rosary Vine

Temperature Average to cool climate, minimum at night 50-55°.

Light Bright, indirect sunshine; good in an east window where sun is not too hot.

Watering Soil may dry out between waterings.

Fertilize Apply at half the recommended strength every 2-4 weeks.

Soil Add an equal volume of peatmoss or shredded sphagnum to a general house plant mix. Must be well drained.

9

Cissus

GRAPE IVY
Cissus rhombifolia

Rambling stems with 3-part compound leaves. Pinch tips to encourage branching. Relatively slow growing.

Caring For Your Cissus

Temperature	Average to warm climate; tolerates minimum at night of 50-55°.
Light	Diffused sunshine or partial shade.
Watering	Keep soil uniformly moist but not wet.
Fertilize	Every 2-3 months.
Soil	Any general house plant mix or soil that permits good drainage.

KANGAROO IVY
Cissus antarctica

Big saw-toothed leaves on flexible stems. This one tolerates dry air, and soil can be allowed to dry between waterings.

CORDATUM
Philodendron oxycardium
Versatile and tolerant trailing or climbing Philodendron. Trim to encourage branching and fresh new growth.

FLORIDA *Philodendron x 'Florida'*
Five-lobed leaves on flexible stems. Pinch tips for full, bushy growth.

Hanging Philodendrons

Caring For Your Philodendron

Temperature Average to warm climate; tolerates minimum at night as low as 50-55°.
Light Bright diffused light, avoid strong sun; tolerates shade.
Watering Keep soil uniformly moist but not wet.
Fertilize Every 3-4 months.
Soil Any general house plant mix or add peatmoss for a more humusy combination.

Japanese Aralia

Fatsia japonica

Maple-like leaves grace this little shrubby plant. Thick flexible stems curve under the foliage weight. This one has more deeply divided leaves than the hybrid x *Fatshedera* (not illustrated).

Caring For Your Fatsia

Temperature	Cool climate, minimum at night 45-55°; tolerates as cool as 40° for short periods.
Light	Partial shade or diffused sunshine; shade outdoors.
Watering	Keep soil uniformly moist but not wet.
Fertilize	Every 4-6 months.
Soil	Any general house plant mix or soil that permits good drainage.

Trailing Ficus

CREEPING FIG ►
Ficus pumila

Creeping, trailing stems root where they touch soil. A free-branching variety, likes fresh air but not drafts.

VARIEGATED ROOTING FIG
Ficus radicans 'Variegata'

Gray-green leaves with creamy variegations on flexible trailing stems. This one prefers a warmer, more humid atmosphere.

Caring For Your Trailing Fig

Temperature Average to warm climate, minimum at night 62-65°; tolerates as cool as 50° for short periods.

Light Diffused sunlight or partial shade; avoid drafts.

Watering Keep soil uniformly moist but not wet.

Fertilize Every 2 months.

Soil Any general house plant mix or soil that permits good drainage.

Hedera

NEEDLEPOINT IVY *Hedera helix 'Needlepoint'*
Slender pointed leaves in formal ranks, on upturned branching stems.

Caring For Your English Ivy

Temperature	Average to cool climate, minimum at night 45-50°.
Light	Full sun or bright indirect light; also tolerates shade.
Watering	Keep soil uniformly moist but not wet.
Fertilize	Every 3-4 months.
Soil	Any general house plant mix or soil that permits good drainage.

ENGLISH IVY *Hedera helix*
Versatile trailer for indoors and out. Some varieties survive even the northern winter.

SWEETHEART IVY *Hedera helix 'Scutifolia'*
An unusual leaf shape for ivy. Trim shoots to encourage bushy development.

Trailing Pothos

MARBLE QUEEN
Scindapsus aureus 'Marble Queen'
Sparkling white marbled effect on smooth foliage. Trailing stems grow indefinitely; trim to contain size and to encourage branching.

DEVIL'S IVY
Scindapsus aureus
Golden variegated vine with waxy leaves; stem roots where it touches soil or in water. Pinch tips to encourage bushiness.

Caring For Your Pothos (Scindapsus)

Temperature	Average to warm climate; minimum at night 62-65°; tolerates lower temperatures (55°) for short periods.
Light	Diffused sunlight or partial shade.
Watering	Soil may dry out between waterings.
Fertilize	Every 3 months.
Soil	Add peatmoss or shredded sphagnum to an equal volume of general house plant mix.

Senecio

VARIEGATED WAX IVY *Senecio macroglossus variegatus*

Spreading, trailing vine with succulent green and cream foliage. Branches prolifically; trim to shape.

Caring For Your German Ivy (Senecio)

Temperature	Average climate, minimum at night 50-60°.
Light	Diffused sunlight or partial shade.
Watering	Keep soil uniformly moist but not wet.
Fertilize	Apply at half the recommended strength every 1-2 months.
Soil	Any general house plant mix or soil that permits good drainage.

GERMAN IVY *Senecio mikanioides*
Fast growing vine with fresh green leaves. Trim to encourage bushiness and to contain size.

Vinca Major

BAND PLANT *Vinca major variegata*
Trails of waxy cream-edged leaves on wiry stems; trim to encourage bushiness. Fine for outdoor use, and to combine with other plants in hanging baskets. Big blue flowers in spring.

Caring For Your Band Plant

Temperature	Average climate, minimum at night 50-55°.
Light	Plenty of light, full sun especially in winter; protect from the heat of summer sun through glass.
Watering	Keep soil uniformly moist but not wet.
Fertilize	Every 1-2 months.
Soil	Any general house plant mix or soil that permits good drainage.

LIPSTICK VINE
Aeschynanthus lobbianus
Trailing stems hang down 1-3 feet, tipped in spring with glistening red blossoms. After flowering, prune shoots back to 6 inches to encourage strong new growth.

Hanging Basket Vines

Caring For Your Basket Vine

Temperature Average to warm climate, minimum at night 62-65°.

Light Plenty of light though shade from full sun in summer and outdoors.

Watering Keep soil uniformly moist but not wet.

Fertilize Every month while making vigorous new growth after flowering. Every other month in fall and winter.

Soil Any good house plant mix, or add peatmoss for a more humusy combination.

ZEBRA BASKET VINE *Aeschynanthus marmoratus*
Big, dark leaves on trailing stems. Vein network is highlighted in yellow, and leaf undersides
are dark red. Spring flowers are green with brown flecks.

Goldfish Vines

SMALL LEAVED GOLDFISH VINE *Columnea microphylla*
Tiny rounded leaves are dwarfed when the orange-red blossoms open.

GOLDFISH PLANT
Columnea linearis

Silky rose pink flowers appear in leaf axils at any time of year.

Caring For Your Columnea

Temperature	Average to warm climate, minimum at night 62-65°.
Light	Plenty of light though shade from full sun in summer and outdoors.
Watering	Keep soil uniformly moist but not wet.
Fertilize	Every month.
Soil	Any good house plant mix, or add peatmoss for a more humusy combination.

CHOCOLATE SOLDIER
Columnea x 'Chocolate Soldier'

Large-leaved hybrid with gleaming foliage on upright and trailing stems.

MAARSEN'S COLUMNEA *Columnea x 'Maarsen's Flame'*
Creamy markings give this trailing epiphyte added appeal.

Caring For Your Columnea: See Page 23

Sturdy Wax Plants

LURA-LEI *Hoya compacta 'Mauna Loa' (Pat. 3054)*
Creamy leaves edged in green make a natural leï on the trailing stems. Light pink flowers in summer.

Caring For Your Hoya: See Page 27

KRIMSON PRINCESS
Hoya carnosa rubra (Pat. 3105)

Smooth waxy leaves are variegated deep pink when young, mature to cream and green. Flowers maroon.

WAX PLANT
Hoya minata

Cascades of rounded velvety leaves characterize this variety. Soft white star-shaped blossom clusters add fragrance to the established plant.

HINDU ROPE *Hoya compacta regalis (Pat. 3306)*
Colorful ropes of crinkled foliage, with deep pink in the younger leaves. Clusters of blossom are maroon.

Caring For Your Hoya

Temperature	Average to warm climate, minimum at night 60-65°; tolerates as cool as 45° for short periods.
Light	Bright indirect light or partial shade; avoid full midday sun.
Watering	Soil may dry out between waterings.
Fertilize	Every 2-3 months.
Soil	Any general house plant mix or soil that permits good drainage.

FAN MAIDENHAIR
Adiantum tenerum 'Wrightii'
Arching fronds overlap in a graceful cascade of fan-like leaflets. New growth is tinged pink.

AUSTRALIAN MAIDENHAIR
Adiantum hispidulum

Spreading five-fingered fronds are borne on slender wiry stems. Young leaves have an attractive pink coloring.

DELTA MAIDENHAIR
Adiantum raddianum 'Pacific Maid'

Sturdy compact plant with ruffled leaflets; the fronds grow 8 to 15 inches long. A tolerant houseplant.

Maidenhair Ferns

Caring For Your Maidenhair Fern

Temperature	Average climate, minimum at night 55-65°; tolerates as cool as 45° for short periods. Best with days 70° or cooler.
Light	Shade from direct sun; good in unbroken north light all year. Needs humid air to prevent leaf edges from turning brown.
Watering	Never allow soil to dry out, though do not saturate it. Where cooler and drier atmosphere prevails in winter when growth is slower, water only enough to prevent wilting.
Fertilize	Apply at half the recommended strength every 4-6 months.
Soil	Add peatmoss, shredded sphagnum, or other humus to a general house plant mix, for a porous woodsy combination.

Asparagus Ferns

ASPARAGUS FERN
Asparagus densiflorus 'Sprengeri'

Cascading stems with charming light green needles. Pinch tips or cut back for new bushy growth.

Caring For Your Asparagus Fern

Temperature	Average climate, minimum at night 55-65°.
Light	Plenty of light though avoid full sun. Good in unbroken north light all year.
Watering	Keep soil uniformly moist but not wet. Stout fleshy roots help Asparagus survive an occasional drought.
Fertilize	Every 3-4 months.
Soil	Any general house plant mix or soil that permits good drainage.

PLUMOSA FERN ▼
Asparagus setaceus

Rich green lace on long twining stems. Cut back older stems to encourage fresh new growth.

MOTHER FERN
Asplenium viviparum

Lacy dark green fronds arch and cascade as new plantlets develop right on the mother plant.

Caring For Your Asplenium Fern

Temperature	Average to cool conditions, minimum at night 50-55°.
Light	Shade from direct sun; good in unbroken north light all year. Needs humid air to prevent leaf edges from turning brown.
Watering	Never allow the soil to dry out, though do not saturate it. Where a cooler and drier atmosphere prevails in winter when growth is slower, water only enough to prevent wilting.
Fertilize	Apply at half the recommended strength every 4-6 months.
Soil	Add peatmoss, shredded sphagnum, or other humus to a general house plant mix for a porous woodsy combination.

BIRDSNEST FERN
Asplenium nidus

A bright and durable fern: the shiny fronds grow up to 3 feet long.

31

Climbing Fern *Lygodium japonicum*

Charming lacy fronds on thread-like stems which twine and cascade.

Caring For Your Climbing Fern

Temperature	Cool location, minimum at night 50-55°.
Light	Shade from direct sun; good in unbroken north light all year. Needs humid air to prevent leaf edges from turning brown.
Watering	Keep soil uniformly moist but not wet.
Fertilize	Apply at half the recommended strength every 4-6 months.
Soil	Any general house plant mix or soil that permits good drainage.

Boston Ferns *Nephrolepis exaltata bostoniensis*

Elegantly arched fronds cascade from the rich green rosette.

Caring For Your Boston Fern: See Page 35

VERONA LACE FERN *Nephrolepis exaltata 'Verona'*
Very lacy fronds with tiny leaflets; trails completely cover the hanging container.

DWARF BOSTON FERN

Nephrolepis exaltata
bostoniensis compacta

Freely clustered fresh green fronds, more upright and compact than Boston Fern.

BOSTON PETTICOAT

Nephrolepis exaltata
'Petticoat'

Frills and ruffles on long fronds make a gracious crinoline effect.

Caring For Your Boston Fern

Temperature	Cool location, minimum at night 50-55°.
Light	Sun in winter, shade in summer; prefers humid air.
Watering	Keep soil uniformly moist but not wet.
Fertilize	Apply at half the recommended strength every 4-6 months.
Soil	Any general house plant mix or soil that permits good drainage.

FLORIDA RUFFLE FERN

Nephrolepis exaltata
'Florida Ruffle'

Dense ruffles on thickly clustered fronds, 18 to 24 inches long.

Staghorn Fern *Platycerium bifurcatum*

Slow growing epiphyte clings to its support with roots behind the shield-like basal segments. Antler-shaped fronds grow to about 3 feet long. The best Staghorn for home conditions.

Caring For Your Staghorn Fern

Temperature	Average to cool location, minimum at night 50-55°. Tolerates as cool as 40° for short periods.
Light	Sun in winter, shade in summer; prefers humid air.
Watering	Keep the root ball uniformly moist but not wet: soak it in the sink at intervals, then allow it to drain before rehanging the fern.
Soil	A porous, humusy mixture, containing Osmunda fern fibers, sphagnum moss, or shredded bark and peatmoss.

Green Cliffbrake *Pellaea viridis*

Gleaming wiry stems and smooth leaflets resemble maidenhair. Bushy habit, fronds up to 2½ feet long.

Caring For Your Green Cliffbrake Fern

Temperature Cool location, minimum at night 50-55°.
Light Shade from direct sun; good in unbroken north light all year.
Watering Keep soil uniformly moist but not wet.
Fertilize Apply at half the recommended strength every 4-6 months.
Soil Any good house plant mix, or add peatmoss for a more humusy soil.

37

Polypody Fern Polypodium scolopendria

Bring in an outdoorsy touch with this woodland fern. Its rhizomes creep along the soil surface, so plant doesn't need a deep container.

Caring For Your Polypody Fern

Temperature Average to warm climate; tolerates minimum at night of 50-55°.
Light Diffused sunlight or partial shade; prefers humid air.
Watering Keep soil uniformly moist but not wet.
Fertilize Apply at half the recommended strength every 4-6 months.
Soil Add peatmoss, shredded sphagnum, or other humus to a general house plant mix for a porous woodsy combination.

Rabbit's Foot Fern Davallia fejeensis

Cascading fronds on wiry stems make this a superb hanging specimen. The brown, wooly rhizome gives this one its name.

Caring For Your Rabbit's Foot Fern

Temperature Average to cool climate, minimum at night 50-60°. Best with days 70° or cooler.
Light Shade from direct sun; good in unbroken north light all year. Prefers humid air. Provide heavy shade out of doors.
Watering Keep soil uniformly moist but not wet.
Fertilize Apply at half the recommended strength every 4-6 months.
Soil Add peatmoss, shredded sphagnum, or other humus to general house plant mix for a porous woodsy combination.

Pyrrosia Fern *Pyrrosia macrocarpa*

Succulent fern with straplike leathery fronds which grow to about 2 feet. Their shining green brightens a dull day.

Caring For Your Pyrrosia Fern

Temperature Average to cool climate, minimum at night 50-55°.

Light Shade from direct sun; good in unbroken north light all year. Prefers humid air.

Watering Keep soil uniformly moist but not wet.

Fertilize Apply at half the recommended strength every 4-6 months.

Soil Add peatmoss, shredded sphagnum, or other humus to a general house plant mix for a porous woodsy combination.

Azalea *Rhododendron hybrid*

A seasonal beauty with flowers that last up to 6 weeks if nights are cool.

Caring For Your Azalea

Temperature	Average to cool climate, minimum at night 50-60°
Light	Bright diffused light; avoid full sun to prevent blossom burn.
Watering	Never allow soil to dry out, though do not saturate it or let the pot stand in water.
Fertilize	None needed while your Azalea is flowering.
Soil	An acid mix of peatmoss with half as much or an equal volume of general house plant mix.
After flowering	Continue to water your Azalea to maintain active growth and feed it every 2-4 weeks with an acid-lovers fertilizer. Give the plant a shaded position out of doors when spring frost danger is past. Trim as desired before mid-July. Bud development begins any time after midsummer. When nights start getting cooler, reduce fertilization to every 4-6 weeks and cut down on watering frequency. Bring the Azalea indoors when freezing temperatures are likely, but maintain it in a cool room to complete bud formation. When flower color shows, the plant can be moved to the warmer area for you to enjoy the new blossoms.

Dauphin Violet *Streptocarpus saxorum*

Delightful mountain plant with pale violet blossoms throughout summer.

Caring For Your Dauphin Violet

Temperature Average climate, minimum at night 60-65°; cooler during the winter months (55-60°)

Light Indirect sunlight or partial shade, full sun in winter.

Watering Keep soil uniformly moist but not wet; avoid splashing water onto foliage. During the cooler winter period, soil may be allowed to dry between waterings.

Fertilize Apply at half the recommended strength every month while growing and flowering.

Soil Any good house plant mix, or add peatmoss for a more humusy and well drained combination.

African Violet *Saintpaulia*

Velvety leaves in spreading rosettes often have red undersides and stems. Single or double blossoms in many hues of blue, pink and white. Flowers at any time of year.

Caring For Your African Violet

Temperature Average to warm climate, minimum at night 60-65°.

Light Indirect sunlight or partial shade; prefers humid air.

Watering Keep soil uniformly moist but not wet; avoid splashing water onto foliage.

Fertilize Apply at half the recommended strength every month.

Soil Add peatmoss to an equal volume of general house plant mix for a humusy and well drained combination.

41

WAX BEGONIA ▲
Begonia semperflorens

Continuous blossom, useful indoors and out. A fibrous rooted begonia whose stem portions root quickly.

▲▼ *Pendulous Begonias* Begonia tuberhybrida pendula

Abundant flowers in many forms and colors.

FUCHSIA BEGONIA ▼
Begonia fuchsioides

Arching stems grow 2 to 3 feet long, bear red, fuchsia-like flowers. A fibrous rooted begonia.

Caring For Your Flowering Begonia

Temperature	Average to cool climate, minimum at night 50-60°
Light	Bright diffused sunlight. Shade outdoors; best in cooler climates.
Watering	Soil may dry slightly between waterings.
Fertilize	Every month.
Soil	Add peatmoss to an equal volume of a general house plant mix for a porous, humusy combination.
After flowering	(Tuberous rooted begonias) Reduce watering frequency as the leaves die back. Lift the tubers and store in a cool (frost-free) and dry, dark place. In late winter, replant and water well to start growth, giving plenty of light. Keep the soil moist. No fertilizer is needed until the first leaves are fully expanded. Begonias can be grown in their flowering location; for outdoor use, start inside and move out when all frost danger is past and nights remain above 40°

Mock Strawberry *Duchesnea indica*

Fast growing strawberry-like plant with yellow blossoms and edible, though tasteless, fruits. Spreads vigorously; leaves remain into winter, and plant regenerates in spring.

Caring For Your Mock Strawberry

Temperature	Cool climate, minimum at night 45-55°
Light	Plenty of bright diffused light, full sun in winter. Partial shade out of doors.
Watering	Keep soil uniformly moist but not wet. Reduce frequency in winter.
Fertilize	Every 2-4 weeks while growing vigorously.
Soil	Any general house plant mix or soil that permits good drainage.

Vigorous trailing plant flowers throughout summer. Remove dead heads for continued blossom.

Ivy Geranium *Pelargonium peltatum*

Caring For Your Ivy Geranium

Temperature	Average to cool climate, minimum at night 45-55°.
Light	Full sun or bright diffused light.
Watering	Soil may dry out between waterings.
Fertilize	Every month during spring and summer.
Soil	Any general house plant mix or soil that permits good drainage.
After flowering	Reduce watering frequency as the leaves die back. Store your geranium in its pot, or shake off the soil and store the roots dry, in a frost-free dark place. Or take cuttings, root and maintain them indoors until spring. Restart stored geraniums in late winter when new growth appears, by gradually increasing water and add fertilizer when growth is well under way.

Brazil Oxalis

Oxalis braziliensis

Pretty rose-pink flowers adorn cheerful green leaves in winter and spring. This Oxalis rests after flowering, then restarts growth in fall.

Caring For Your Oxalis

Temperature	Average to cool climate, minimum at night 50-60°.
Light	Plenty of light, full sun; partial shade out of doors.
Watering	Soil may dry out between waterings; reduce frequency after flowering when plant rests.
Fertilize	Every month while growing vigorously.
Soil	Any general house plant mix or soil that permits good drainage.

Busy Lizzie

Impatiens walleriana sultanii
Easy to flower charmer for indoors or out.
Available in a variety of colors.

Caring For Your Busy Lizzie

Temperature Average to cool climate, minimum at night 50-60°.
Light Bright indirect light or full sun; partial shade out of doors.
Watering Keep soil uniformly moist but not wet.
Fertilize Every 2-4 weeks while growing vigorously.
Soil Add peatmoss to an equal volume of a general house plant mix for a porous, humusy combination.

Black-Eyed Susan *Thunbergia alata*

Perennial vine often grown as an annual for outdoor use. Plant or sow in summer for winter blossom indoors. Prune back older stems to soil level to encourage new growth.

Caring For Your Black-Eyed Susan

Temperature Average climate, minimum at night 50-60°.
Light Plenty of light.
Watering Keep soil uniformly moist but not wet.
Fertilize Every 2-4 weeks while growing vigorously.
Soil Any general house plant mix or soil that permits good drainage.

45

Lovely Browallia *Browallia speciosa major*

Cascading and spreading habit ideal for hanging containers. An annual in shades of blue and white; sow seed in summer for winter displays, or in late winter for summer decoration.

Caring For Your Lovely Browallia

Temperature — Average climate, minimum at night 55-60°.

Light — Diffused light or partial shade in summer, full sun in winter. Shade out of doors.

Watering — Keep soil uniformly moist but not wet.

Fertilize — Every 2-4 weeks.

Soil — Add peatmoss to an equal volume of a general house plant mix for a porous, humusy combination.

Trailing Lobelia *Lobelia erinus and hybrids*

Fast growing pendulous annual with tiny blue flowers in profusion all summer. Superb for outdoor displays.

Caring For Your Trailing Lobelia

Temperature — Average to cool climate, minimum at night 50-55°.

Light — Indirect sunlight or partial shade; tolerates full sun in the north.

Watering — Keep soil uniformly moist but not wet.

Fertilize — Every 2-4 weeks.

Soil — Add peatmoss to an equal volume of a general house plant mix for a porous, humusy combination.

Petunia *Petunia x hybrida*

Sparkling blossoms for full sun; an annual that can be flowered in winter from summer sowings. Late winter sown plants flower throughout summer.

Caring For Your Petunia

Temperature	Average to cool climate, minimum at night 45-55°.
Light	Full sun.
Watering	Soil may dry out between waterings.
Fertilize	Every 2-4 weeks.
Soil	Any general house plant mix or soil that permits good drainage.

BEGONIA *Begonia acetosa*

Big soft leaves on long stems spread in the loose rosette. Grows from a rhizome.

REX BEGONIA *Begonia rex*

Colorful foliage in many-hued variety. Superb to hang indoors and out.

FERN BEGONIA *Begonia foliosa 'Babylon Lace'*
Tiny leaves give the fern-like appeal to this pendulous plant.
Small pinkish blossoms.

Fancy-Leaved Begonias

Caring For Your Fancy-Leaved Begonia

Temperature	Average to warm climate, minimum at night 60-65°.
Light	Bright diffused sunlight, shade outdoors; prefers humid air.
Watering	Keep soil uniformly moist but not wet.
Fertilize	Apply at half the recommended strength every month.
Soil	Rich and humusy, must have good drainage. Add peatmoss to an equal volume of a general house plant mix.

SILVER JEWEL BEGONIA

Begonia x 'Silver Jewel'
A magnificent hybrid with silvery blisters on the sturdy leaves.

49

SPIDER PLANT
Chlorophytum elatum 'Vittatum'
Clusters of green foliage with lighter midribs. Long cascades of new plantlets remain for years on the parent plant.

PICTURATUM
Chlorophytum comosum 'Picturatum'
Loose rosettes of grasslike leaves with creamy yellow and green stripes. 'Spiders' form on flower stalks.

Spider Plants

Caring For Your Spider Plant

Temperature Average climate, minimum at night 50-55°.
Light Diffused sunlight or partial shade; good in unbroken north light all year.
Watering Keep soil uniformly moist but not wet. Sensitive to fluorides (see page 6).
Fertilize Every 2 months.
Soil Any general house plant mix or soil that permits good drainage.

◄ **SPIDER PLANT** *Chlorophytum comosum 'Vittatum'*
White-banded leaves in gracefully curving clusters. Long flowering stems will develop new plantlets.

ACAJOU
Episcia cupreata 'Acajou'

Silvery leaves with mahogany markings fill the container to overflowing. Orange-red blossoms in summer.

CHOCOLATE SOLDIER
Episcia cupreata 'Chocolate Soldier'

Quilted chocolaty leaves mound 6-12 inches and spread over the basket's edge. Gay red flowers in summer.

MOSS AGATE
Episcia 'Moss Agate'

Puckered green leaves spread informally, provide an attractive foil for the crimson flowers.

Caring For Your Episcia

Temperature Average to warm climate, minimum at night 60-65°.
Light Bright indirect light; prefers humid air.
Watering Keep soil uniformly moist but not wet; avoid splashing water onto foliage.
Fertilize Every 4-6 weeks.
Soil Add peatmoss to an equal volume of general house plant mix for a humusy and well drained combination.

Flame Violets

PINK BROCADE
Episcia 'Pink Brocade'

Vivid pink contrasts the silvery gray leaf centers of this mounding, spreading plant. Brilliant orange flowers in summer.

Silver Nerved Fittonia

Fittonia verschaffeltii argyroneura

Spreading branches grow beyond the container's edge; the silvery-white etched foliage makes this a pleasing decorator item.

Caring For Your Fittonia

Temperature	Average to warm climate, minimum at night 62-65°.
Light	Diffused sunlight or unbroken north light; prefers humid air.
Watering	Keep soil uniformly moist but not wet.
Fertilize	Apply at half the recommended strength every 1-2 months.
Soil	Any general house plant mix or soil that permits good drainage.

Purple Passion Vine

Gynura 'Sarmentosa'

Easy-care irridescent velvety vine with purple color. Fast growing; prune to encourage bushiness. Color lost with insufficient light.

Caring For Your Gynura

Temperature	Average to warm climate, minimum at night 62-65°.
Light	Full sun, thrives in bright light.
Watering	Keep soil uniformly moist but not wet.
Fertilize	Every month.
Soil	Any general house plant mix or soil that permits good drainage.

Purple Waffle Plant

Hemigraphis 'Exotica'

Trailing stems with irregularly puckered leaves give the Waffle Plant an informal appeal. Leaf undersides and stems are wine red.

Caring For Your Waffle Plant

Temperature Average to warm climate, minimum at night 62-65°.

Light Thrives in shade with no direct sun.

Watering Keep soil uniformly moist but not wet.

Fertilize Every 1-2 months.

Soil Any general house plant mix or soil that permits good drainage.

Polka Dot Plant

Hypoestes sanguinolenta

Spreading and erect stems bear soft green foliage dotted with rosy pink speckles. A fast growing tropical herb; take cuttings for renewed plants.

Caring For Your Polka Dot Plant

Temperature Average to warm climate, minimum at night 60-70°.

Light Bright filtered light, avoid strong sun and drafts.

Watering Keep soil uniformly moist but not wet.

Fertilize Apply at half the recommended strength every 1-2 months. Plants are easily restarted from cuttings, every one or two years.

Soil Add peatmoss to an equal volume of general house plant mix for a humusy, well drained combination.

55

Zebra Plants

ZEBRA PLANT
Calathea zebrina

Bold and vigorous, ideal for use outdoors, with shade, in summer. Leaf undersides and stems are purplish red.

Caring For Your Zebra Plant

Temperature	Average to warm climate, minimum at night 62-65°.
Light	Diffused sunlight or partial shade, shade outdoors; prefers humid air.
Watering	Keep soil uniformly moist but not wet.
Fertilize	Apply at half the recommended strength every 2-4 weeks.
Soil	Add an equal volume of peatmoss to a general house plant mix.

ZEBRA PLANT
Calathea roseo-picta

Darker foliage indicates need for heavier shade from full sun. Good spreading habit for hanging basket use.

Prayer Plant *Maranta leuconeura massangeana*

Conversation piece with leaves that fold up at night, displaying wine red undersides. Roots easily at the nodes.

Caring For Your Prayer Plant

Temperature   Average to warm climate, minimum at night 62-65°; tolerates lower temperatures (55°) for short periods.

Light   Shade or diffused sunlight; prefers humid air.

Watering   Keep soil uniformly moist but not wet. Sensitive to fluorides (see page 6).

Fertilize   Every 1-2 months.

Soil   Any general house plant mix or soil that permits good drainage.

57

Moneywort — Creeping Jenny

Lysimachia nummularia

Dense spreading creeper with nearly circular leaves. Sometimes used as ground cover outdoors. Makes excellent hanging plant.

Caring For Your Lysimachia

Temperature	Very hardy, withstands low temperatures well.
Light	Diffused sunlight or partial shade.
Watering	Keep soil uniformly moist but not wet.
Fertilize	Every 2 months.
Soil	Any general house plant mix or soil that permits good drainage.

CREEPING PILEA, 'BABY TEARS' ►
Pilea depressa

Masses of minute light green leaves on fleshy creeping and trailing stems. Branches freely, roots wherever stem touches soil.

Caring For Your Pilea

Temperature	Average to warm climate, minimum at night 60-65°
Light	Diffused sunlight or partial shade.
Watering	Keep soil uniformly moist but not wet.
Fertilize	Every 2 months.
Soil	Any general house plant mix or soil that permits good drainage.

Pilea for Hanging Containers

ALUMINUM PLANT
Pilea cadierei

Silvery markings on the quilted leaves give this one its name. Pinch tips to encourage branching.

FRIENDSHIP PLANT
Pilea involucrata

Durable, spreading yet close-set plant. Leaves are green when grown in shade, coppery in light.

59

WATERMELON BEGONIA
Pellionia daveauana

Spreading and trailing stems make an attractive hanging display of patterned leaves.

Pellionia

SATIN PELLIONIA
Pellionia pulchra

Reticulate vein pattern highlights the close-set foliage; pinkish creeping stems.

Caring For Your Pellionia

Temperature	Average to warm climate, minimum at night 60-65°.
Light	Shade or diffused light.
Watering	Keep soil uniformly moist but not wet.
Fertilize	Apply at half the recommended strength every 1-2 months.
Soil	Any general house plant mix or soil that permits good drainage.

Saffron Pepper Piper crocatum

Picturesque vine to trail or climb; twining stems grow 3 to 5 feet long. The pink-veined leaves have purple colored undersides.

Caring For Your Saffron Pepper

Temperature Average to warm climate, minimum at night 60-65°.

Light Bright diffused light, shade from direct sun; prefers humid air.

Watering Keep soil uniformly moist but not wet.

Fertilize Apply at half the recommended strength every 1-2 months.

Soil Add peatmoss to an equal volume of general house plant mix for a humusy, well drained combination.

PEPPER FACE *Peperomia obtusifolia*
Blunt-tipped waxy leaves are faintly cupped; fleshy stems bow and trail under the weight of the foliage.

PRINCESS ASTRID *Peperomia orba*
Spoon shaped leaves have distinct midribs and short stems. A low, spreading variety.

PROSTRATE PEPEROMIA
Peperomia prostrata
Tiny creeping plant has circular leaves, beautifully marked with silver on a brownish-green base.

3-NERVED PEPEROMIA
Peperomia trinervis
Vigorous spreading creeper with distinctly three-nerved leaves on red stems.

Caring For Your Peperomia

Temperature　Average to warm climate, minimum at night 60-65°.
Light　Indirect sunlight or partial shade.
Watering　Keep soil uniformly moist but not wet.
Fertilize　Apply at half the recommended strength every 2 months.
Soil　Any general house plant mix or soil that permits good drainage.

◄ **GREEN PEPEROMIA** *Peperomia viridis*
Intense green foliage on sprawling and erect fleshy stems.

63

CUPID
PEPEROMIA
*Peperomia
scandens
'Variegata'*
Trails of fleshy green-
and-cream leaves on
pale stems that become
tinted red in light.

Swedish Ivy

VARIEGATED SWEDISH IVY *Plectranthus oertendahlii 'Variegatus'* ▲

Creamy white variegations on green leaves, irregular and variable markings. Square stems are reddish-purple.

Caring For Your Swedish Ivy

Temperature   Average climate, tolerates minimum at night as cool as 50°.
Light   Diffused sunshine or partial shade.
Watering   Keep soil uniformly moist but not wet.
Fertilize   Apply at half the recommended strength every 1-2 months.
Soil   Any general house plant mix or soil that permits good drainage.

SWEDISH IVY
Plectranthus australis

Fast growing plant with waxy leaves on fleshy spreading stems. Small white flowers cluster on erect stems.

PURPLE-LEAVED SWEDISH IVY ►
Plectranthus purpuratus

Spreading, creeping herb with hairy leaves, purplish undersides. Small lavender colored flowers.

65

Strawberry Begonia *Saxifraga sarmentosa*

Informal plant spreads with new plantlets on runners, like strawberries. Erect stems bear clusters of white blossoms in summer.

Caring For Your Saxifrage

Temperature	Average to cool climate, minimum at night 40-50°.
Light	Diffused sun or bright indirect light; full sun in winter. Give partial shade outdoors.
Watering	Soil may dry out between waterings.
Fertilize	Every 3-4 months.
Soil	Any general house plant mix or soil that permits good drainage.

Piggyback Plant *Tolmiea menziesii*

Big fresh green leaves on long stems form a widespreading rosette. New plants develop at the base of every leaf, root quickly even in water.

Caring For Your Piggyback Plant

Temperature	Cool climate, minimum at night 45-50°; tolerates colder temperatures for short periods.
Light	Bright indirect light, full sun in winter.
Watering	Keep soil uniformly moist but not wet.
Fertilize	Every 2 months.
Soil	Any general house plant mix or soil that permits good drainage.

Teddy Bear Vine *Cyanotis kewensis*

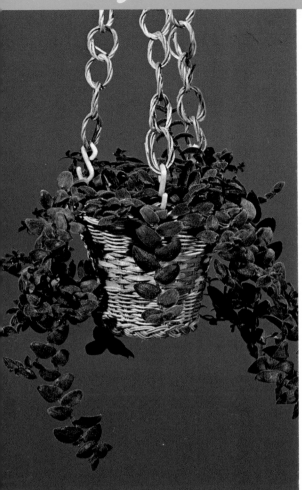

Furry trailing vine with upturned stem tips. Leaves have purplish undersides. Violet-blue flowers.

Caring For Your Teddy Bear Vine

Temperature	Average climate, minimum at night 50-55°.
Light	Full sun or bright diffused light.
Watering	Soil may dry out between waterings.
Fertilize	Apply at half the recommended strength every 1-2 months.
Soil	Any general house plant mix or soil that permits good drainage.

Tahitian Bridal Veil *Gibasis geniculata* ▶

Freely branching, dense growth with slender flexible stems and friendly green leaves, undersides purple. Clouds of tiny white blossoms give this plant its name.

Caring For Your Gibasis

Temperature	Warm climate, minimum at night 60-65°.
Light	Diffused sunlight or partial shade.
Watering	Soil may dry out between waterings.
Fertilize	Apply at half the recommended strength every 1-2 months.
Soil	Any general house plant mix or soil that permits good drainage.

Moses in the Cradle

Rhoeo spathacea

Thick, flexible stems densely clothed with stiff leaves, spreading and trailing from the container. Tiny white blossoms open at the leaf bases.

Caring For Your Moses in the Cradle

Temperature	Average climate, minimum at night 50-55°.
Light	Diffused sunlight or partial shade.
Watering	Keep soil uniformly moist but not wet.
Fertilize	Every 3-4 months.
Soil	Any general house plant mix or soil that permits good drainage.

Purple Heart

Setcreasea purpurea

Strong trailing plant, useful for outdoor decoration in summer. Purple color develops in sun or strong light.

Caring For Your Purple Heart

Temperature	Average climate, minimum at night 50-60°.
Light	Full sun or bright diffused light.
Watering	Soil may dry out between waterings.
Fertilize	Apply at half the recommended strength every month.
Soil	Any general house plant mix or soil that permits good drainage.

GIANT WHITE INCH PLANT *Tradescantia albiflora 'Albo-vittata'*
Fast growing fleshy stems with striped leaves. Trim the long trails to encourage branching; easy to root in soil or water.

Tradescantia

Caring For Your Tradescantia

Temperature Average climate, minimum at night 50-55°.
Light Plenty of light though avoid strong sun.
Watering Soil may dry out between waterings.
Fertilize Apply at half the recommended strength every 1-2 months.
Soil Any general house plant mix or soil that permits drainage.

VARIEGATED WANDERING JEW

Tradescantia fluminensis 'Variegata'

Friendly green-and-cream candy stripes on fast growing trailing stems. Trim long shots as desired; roots well in soil or water.

BRONZE WANDERING JEW ►
Zebrina purpusii

Faint green stripes on broad brown-purple leaves. Trim off extra long stems and root tips in soil or water.

Caring For Your Wandering Jew (Zebrina)

Temperature	Average climate, minimum at night 50-60°.
Light	Diffused light, avoid strong sun; prefers humid air.
Watering	Keep soil uniformly moist but not wet.
Fertilize	Apply at half the recommended strength every 1-2 months.
Soil	Any general house plant mix or soil that permits good drainage.

TRICOLOR WANDERING JEW ►
Zebrina pendula 'Discolor'

Silver bands on green and purple striped leaves characterize this variety. Grows rapidly, regular trimming maintains bushiness.

◄ WANDERING JEW
Zebrina pendula

Fast growing trails of silver-banded leaves with glowing purple undersides. Trim to encourage branching.

73

Ghost Plant

Graptopetalum paraguayense

Long lived succulent with sprawling, trailing stems. Rosettes of silvery gray brittle leaves. Also known as *Sedum weinbergii*.

Caring For Your Ghost Plant

Temperature Average to cool climate, minimum at night 50-60°. Tolerates lower or higher temperatures, 40 to 100°.

Light Plenty of light, full sun.

Watering Soil may dry out between waterings.

Fertilize Every 3-4 months.

Soil Any general house plant mix or soil that permits good drainage.

Drunkard's Dream *Hatiora salicornioides*

Heavily branched epiphytic member of the cactus family, an interesting conversation item with bottle-shaped branchlets.

Caring For Your Drunkard's Dream

Temperature Average to warm climate, minimum at night 62-65°.

Light Partial shade or diffused sunlight; shade out of doors.

Watering Keep soil uniformly moist but not wet.

Fertilize Every 3-4 months.

Soil Add peatmoss or shredded sphagnum to an equal volume of a general house plant mix for a porous, humusy combination.

Rhipsalis

MISTLETOE CACTUS
Rhipsalis cassutha

Long slender branching strands cascade from the container. Creamy flowers and white mistletoe-like berries.

Caring For Your Rhipsalis

Temperature	Average to warm climate, minimum at night 62-65°.
Light	Partial shade or diffused sunlight; shade out of doors.
Watering	Keep soil uniformly moist but not wet.
Fertilize	Every 3-4 months.
Soil	Add shredded sphagnum or peatmoss to an equal volume of a general house plant mix for a porous, humusy combination.

Rhipsalis clavata

Club-shaped joints form these long pendulous branches. A white flowered species.

Rhipsalis rhombea

Flat leaflike joints make up the flexible branches of this cactus. Cream colored blossoms.

BURRO'S TAIL
Sedum morganianum
Slow growing pendulous stems are clad with gray-green teardrop leaves. Fine indoors and out.

Caring For Your Sedum

Temperature   Average to cool climate, minimum at night 50-60°. Tolerates lower or higher temperatures, 40 to 100°.

Light   Plenty of light, full sun.

Watering   Soil may dry out between waterings.

Fertilize   Every 3-4 months.

Soil   Any general house plant mix or soil that permits good drainage.

Sedum

CHRISTMAS CHEERS
Sedum rubrotinctum
A spreading, branching succulent with blunt fleshy leaves that turn coppery in sunlight.

Disorders of Plants Indoors

Hanging plants are subject to the same conditions encountered by every container-growing plant indoors. The reasons for plant disorders often seem conflicting; for example, a wilting plant can be caused by too much water or too little. If something is amiss with your plant, first check the soil; this is your guide to the most frequent troubles. Less often are the problems caused by too much or too little light: and other plant troubles are brought on by very dry air (usually in winter), hot or cold drafts, insufficient fertilizer, and a potbound root system.

Disorder	Possible causes

PETAL & LEAF TIPS TURN BROWN	Check soil:
	     if DRY, water more often or more thoroughly
	     if MOIST, cause may be high salts: LEACH soil
	 Air too dry

LEAVES TURN YELLOW OR BROWN	Check soil:
	     if DRY, water more often or more thoroughly
	     if MOIST, cause may be high salts: LEACH soil
	     if WET, may be poor drainage or simply overwatering
	 Temperature too high
	 Air too dry
	 Insufficient fresh air

BROWN SPOTS ON PETALS & LEAVES	Overwatering or poor drainage Light too bright
FLOWERS & LEAVES CURL UP	Hot or cold draft
FLOWERS & LEAVES FALL OFF	Overwatering or poor drainage Insufficient light Soil very dry Cold draft Injury caused by manufactured gas
LEAVES PALE GREEN OR YELLOW	Too little or too much light Plant needs fertilizer Temperature too high
NEW GROWTH THIN AND PALE	Too little light Too much nitrogen (N) in fertilizer Temperature too high
NEW LEAVES SMALL	Plant needs repotting—check roots Plant needs fertilizer Injury caused by hight salts: LEACH soil Temperature too high

PLANT WILTS	Check soil:
	     if DRY, water more often or more thoroughly
	     if MOIST, cause may be high salts: LEACH soil
	     if WET, may be poor drainage or simply overwatering
	 Plant needs repotting—check roots
	 Air too dry

WHOLE PLANT SUDDENLY COLLAPSES	Roots dead, caused by water saturation and/or high salts Cold or hot draft
GROWTH STUNTED	Roots dying, caused by water saturation and/or high salts
ROOTS APPEAR ON SOIL SURFACE	Roots may be waterlogged or completely dry in lower part of container Plant needs repotting—check roots
PLANT ROTS AT OR JUST ABOVE SOIL LEVEL	Too much water, caused by overwatering or poor drainage Too cold

To LEACH: see Soluble Salts and Leaching, page 6

The most common indoor pests are spider mites, mealy bugs, scale insects, whitefly and aphids. The use of plant material for outdoor as well as indoor decoration exposes them to all manner of garden pests, such as caterpillars, slugs, snails and thrips, many of which thrive once the plants are moved back indoors. For this reason, plants which are being moved from the outdoor scene to your home should be washed thoroughly with a spray of clear water.

Despite the best control programs employed by growers and retailers, it sometimes happens that a new plant harbors pests whose eggs have survived to hatch in your home conditions. A period of isolation (10-14 days) may be the answer. Yet some pests may not show up for a longer time, being present in minute numbers until the indoor climate becomes more favorable; for example, spider mites thrive in dry air, so they may not become evident until the humid season is past.

Regular and frequent checking for abnormal growth and insects can be combined with your checks for watering needs. Most pests lurk under leaves and close to the growing tip where tissue is softest, and most of them can be washed off with a spray of water. Several washes over a period of two or three weeks, plus isolation for the infested plant to prevent the pest skipping to others, generally eliminates the problem. Chemical sprays are not pleasant to use, and are recommended for outdoor application only if possible. Those sold in aerosol form are hazardous, not only to the general environment, but to the plant tissue which will be burned by the propellant if the nozzle is held too close: a distance of 24 inches should be safe. Ferns are super-sensitive to all forms of chemical spray, and infested fronds are best removed and destroyed.

Diseases are rare for indoor plants, and the only ones likely to be encountered are Botrytis, the gray mold fungus that invades dead and dying tissues, and soft leaf spot or crown rot fungi which thrive in moist atmospheres. The best cure is to remove affected parts, and avoid splashing the plant when you water; give more space for air circulation, or move infected plants to a drier place.

Pest	Typical damage	Control
SPIDER MITES	Tiny white or yellow spots on leaves, later becoming mottled and dusty. Fine webs under leaves and in growing tips. Leaves may curl up. Thrive in dry climates.	Wash and spray plant with clean warm water, several times in 2-3 weeks. Spray Kelthane or Dimite.
SCALE INSECTS	Clusters of green to brown scales under leaves and on stems, plus mottling of foliage when seen against the light.	Rub off the scales, or wipe over with cotton soaked in rubbing alcohol (check plant for tolerance by treating one leaf, then wait 24 hours)—this kills adult insects. Spray Malathion or Nicotine.
MEALY BUGS	Cottony white secretions along stems and under leaves. Flat insects move, though slowly.	Wash off insects and secretions with clean warm water. Kill by wiping off with rubbing alcohol—first check plant's tolerance. Spray Malathion or Nicotine.
WHITE FLIES	Tiny white moths fly up when plant is disturbed; larvae suck plant juices, causing general weakening. Thrive in dry climates, generally on flowering plants and annuals.	Wash off the tiny wingless larvae. Adult whitefly controlled with spray of Malathion.
APHIDS	Greenish insects visibly sucking plant juices, cause small, distorted, weak growth.	Wash whole plant several times. Spray Malathion or Nicotine.

Common Name Index

Botanical Name Index